BOUNCE BACK!

TURNING TRIALS INTO TRIUMPHS

Grateful Rachel

BOUNCE BACK!

TURNING TRIALS INTO TRIUMPHS

Copyright © 2017 by Grateful Rachel

All rights reserved. No part of this book may be reproduced, stored in a retrieval system, or transmitted in any form or by any means — electronic, photocopy, or recorded, without the prior written consent of the author, as it is strictly prohibited. Excerpts and links may be used, provided that full and clear credit is given to the author with specific direction to the original content.

If you would like to use material from the book for short quotations or occasional page copying for personal or group study, it is permitted and encouraged (other than for review purposes), however, prior written permission must be obtained on request by contacting the publisher. Thank you for your respect of the author's rights.

ISBN - 978-1-78808-228-0
Published in the United Kingdom
Published by Women Empowering Projects

TABLE OF CONTENTS

ACKNOWLEDGEMENT v
INTRODUCTION 1

CHAPTER 1: MY STORY 5
CHAPTER 2: MINDSETS MATTER 15
CHAPTER 3: LOVING YOURSELF 26
CHAPTER 4: A LIFE OF SIGNIFICANCE 35
CHAPTER 5: NAVIGATING DIFFERENT SEASONS OF LIFE 42
CHAPTER 6: SUPPORT SYSTEM 51
CHAPTER 7: FORGIVENESS 57
CHAPTER 8: SINGLE PARENTING 66
CHAPTER 9: MAINTAINING FAITH DURING
                 CHALLENGES 76
CHAPTER 10: EMOTIONAL WELLBEING 85

CONCLUSION 108
ABOUT THE AUTHOR 110

DEDICATION

This book is dedicated to my two amazing boys, Christopher and Ethan, who come first whenever I count my blessings. In times of adversity, you give me the strength to stand strong and fight. My life is beautiful because it has you in it; it's a privilege to be your mum.

ACKNOWLEDGEMENT

I want to acknowledge God who has been faithful and without whom I wouldn't have come this far in life; His grace and mercy have seen me through.

I will like to thank my dear mother, Mrs Victoria Opeyokun, for her endless prayers, encouragement, and support. Thank you for believing in me and my God-given vision.

To my siblings, Elizabeth, Christina, Victor, Grace, and Deborah, you are simply the best. Your support over the years has been phenomenal and I am proud to call you my own.

Some friends stick closer than brothers; Shola Alabi is one of such. I am grateful for the day we met many years ago. Your encouragement while working on this book is greatly appreciated.

To my dear friend, Amanda, where do I start? Thank you so much for your input in this book, you are selfless in your giving. I pray you are rewarded accordingly.

Temi Koleowo, my dear girlfriend. Thank you for believing in my passion from the onset and for working with me to package it so it can be a blessing to many. You are truly awesome.

I say a big thank you to my friends, Doyin, Tolu, Bisi and Abby. Your support and encouragement are greatly appreciated. You are all dependable and for this, I am grateful to God.

To my dear Godmother, Dr Titi Osoba, thank you for writing the last chapter of this book. Your prayers and support over the years have gone a long way. I appreciate your role in my life.

To my publisher, Pastor Tunj Ogunjimi, thank you for making this dream a reality.

INTRODUCTION

I truly believe we all have stories to tell and that we can use them to be a blessing to others. In taking the time to share our stories, we can, with them, impact the lives of people around us. Our stories will be able to really touch other lives.

I have put my heart into writing this book in as transparent a manner as possible because I know my story will encourage, inspire, and motivate you. As you turn the pages, I want you to journey with me and share in my triumphs that were preceded by trials. I want to teach you how I brought that old saying, "turning lemons into lemonade," to life because that is what I've done. I have *bounced back* stronger than ever.

My message to you is that you can live your life to the fullest, regardless of your past or present circumstances. I have learnt that each challenge, setback, or disappointment in life either breaks you or makes you a better person.

This has certainly been my own story. I have used the challenges in my life as a stepping stone. I have decided to leave my past behind and look forward to a greater future. I have chosen not to allow my past to limit me, but instead, to push me into becoming a better version of me. It has not been easy, but it has been worth it.

This book will empower you and teach you what you can do in order to bounce back from life's defeats. I found the courage to do so after a difficult childhood and a broken marriage. In this book, I have outlined what I did and what I still do to turn my trials into triumphs.

We all have the ability to choose to make the best of the challenging situations in our lives. I have evolved into a whole woman because my trials have helped me rediscover who I am as a person. As a result, I am no longer broken and I know that as I share my story and the lessons I have learnt, you can also be empowered to be the person you were created to be. I know how difficult it is to be faced with challenges, but trust me when I tell you there are solutions, some of which are in this book. If you are willing to put in the work, then you can fulfil your desire to change your circumstances. You too can walk in freedom and live out your purpose.

I can tell you with boldness and confidence that I have regained my inner glow. I have rediscovered an inner strength and this started when I decided not to allow my circumstances control me, but instead, to start to embrace that which empowers me and gives me the strength to excel.

Life has taught me the importance of inner reflection. Changing our circumstances starts first with changing what goes on within – our perceptions and our thoughts. We need to address the negative mindsets, wrong beliefs, or views that may be holding us bound. The truth is you are the only obstacle in your path with the ability to halt your progress. I had the privilege of getting my Godmother, Dr Titi Osoba, a Consultant Psychiatrist, to write the last chapter of this book on how to understand and manage our emotions in order to survive setbacks and challenges. Her wealth of knowledge and experience on this topic are vast and this will shed more light on this area of our lives. I hope that after you read this book you have the help and support you need to bounce back. There is so much to glean from this book and so I encourage you to take your time while reading it. Read it slowly and get a journal to take some notes. Take time to reflect and spend time getting to know who you are; ask yourself those difficult questions. These are small steps that will have a big impact.

TURNING TRIALS INTO TRIUMPHS

The honest truth is that it is not going to be easy because change takes time and effort, but the rewards are truly awesome. Also, this journey is an on-going one and will take time; we will continue to learn every day as we will be faced with new challenges, however, what you will learn in this book are the right strategies to cope with those challenges as they arise.

I thank you for taking the time to read this book and to invest in your personal growth. Make a commitment to yourself to start and finish strong. I guarantee that this book will change your life in a wonderful way.

You are worth it,

Grateful Rachel.

1

MY STORY

I grew up without my parents. Initially, I thought the only one missing was my dad, but the much I knew as a young child was that, I had my mum and my sisters with me; I had somehow just accepted that I didn't have a dad. I was truly grateful for the family I had, yet, there was an odd longing I couldn't explain—that unshakeable feeling that something was not quite right.

One day, a conversation with my eldest sister, Elizabeth, who was 11 years old at the time, confirmed my worst fears and changed my life for good. I would never forget the emotions I felt when she told me, "Mum is actually our grandma." I was in shock. What had I just heard?

TURNING TRIALS INTO TRIUMPHS

What had she just whispered in my ear? I couldn't believe it. I was so confused, so afraid, so alone. I was sure it was a joke, but no, it wasn't. As the story began to unfold, I realised that everything my sister had told me was true.

My father had left Nigeria for England to seek a better future for us all. At the time he left, my mother was pregnant with me. When I was only 6 months old, my mum left my 2 older sisters – Elizabeth (age 3) and Christina (age 2) – and I, with our paternal grandmother in Nigeria, and left to join our dad in the UK. Life on his own was hard and she needed to go and support him. They were only supposed to be gone for a few years, but a few years ended up being more than a decade.

I was only eight years old when the truth about my life began to unfold and I cried many bitter tears; it was such a painful experience for me. I wasn't really sure what hurt most, the fact that my family was away or that it had been a secret for so long. I longed for them, I wasn't even upset with them. I wasn't angry, I just wanted to be with my family. Now that I knew, I could not fill the void. I dreamt many nights of being reunited with them. I wanted to experience the love of a father and the warmth of a mother; I wanted to be embraced.

My grandma was amazing; she raised us the best way she could. She had her own trauma of losing a husband she loved so much, yet she rose to the challenge and became the mum we needed. I found out that my grandmother even breastfed me. That was difficult. I guess as a young 6-month-old baby looking for comfort, grandma gave me the comfort I needed; I owe a lot to her. I pray her soul continues to rest in perfect peace.

Once I knew the truth, life changed for me in many ways. There were so many unanswered questions that plagued my young, wounded heart. Beyond the void I felt, were the endless questions that always started with WHO? Who were my real parents? Why did they leave me? Didn't they want me? Yet, there was no one to turn to, no one to answer those questions. I couldn't even ask my sisters who were, probably, wondering the same things.

I lived with these painful emotions and over the next 24 months, the unanswered questions piled up. However, my greatest joy and surprise was that two years after my whole world changed, my parents came to Nigeria to visit. I experienced unimaginable joy; it was inexplicable. I couldn't believe I finally got to meet them. I was over the moon and beside myself with excitement. But, I couldn't connect with them because, to me, they felt like total strangers. They were people I had not seen or spoken to before. This was long before the time of easy communication; there were no phones to call, and there was no FaceTime or Skype. So, to me, they were total strangers, but strange as it may sound, I was happy. It was such great news to find out I had three younger siblings – Victor, Grace, and Deborah – but at the same time, I was sad that I had not met them. When my parents had to go back to care for my siblings after staying for only a short while, a fresh wave of pain came over me; watching them leave was a painful experience. I was only ten years old.

Five years later, my older sisters were leaving me too, to join our parents in the UK. They had finished their secondary school education and I was left behind to finish mine. I was now alone in Nigeria with my grandmother; every member of my immediate family was away in the UK. On some nights, I cried as the pain of loneliness enveloped me, yet I found strength in knowing that I would soon finish secondary school and join them. I was counting the seconds, the minutes, and the days as they went by; I couldn't wait.

It was 1990, I was 17 years old, fresh out of secondary school and it was my time to leave. Excitement bubbled within me as I left to join my family. Finally, we will be complete. Finally, we could be the one big, happy family I had always dreamed about. For the very first time, I felt a sense of belonging, I felt liberated. What I didn't anticipate was that my joy would be short-lived. Death knocked on our door so suddenly. Oh my! How cruel life was, I thought. Only seven months of peace, only six months of my father's love and then, he was gone. My heart shattered into a million pieces.

I was just 17 years old and I had only experienced the company of my father for less than a year. I was in such pain and despair. Once again, I had so many unanswered questions. How could this have happened? How can this be? Again, I was faced with so many unanswered questions and somehow, no one understood my pain, no one understood my loss. Everyone else had more time with my dad, they all got to know him for longer than I did. I felt robbed. I felt cheated. I felt so lonely.

In the midst of all the pain, I found God. Well, actually, God found me, and His timing was perfect. He knew what I needed and He filled me with calmness and peace, and I held on to Him for dear life because He was all I had. His grace saved me and was a balm to my broken heart.

TURNING TRIALS INTO TRIUMPHS

Two years after my dad died, I met a wonderful man and some sunshine came into my life. I was young and in love. In him, I found the closure I needed, the protection I wanted, the love of a man that I craved but never got from my dad. I was so excited when he asked me to marry him, and three years later, I became his wife. My dad's death taught me the value of time so I was determined to have a stable home and I vowed to give my children the love and affection I never had, growing up. I knew I would do things in a different way. We would be a close-knit family; my children would always have mum and dad, and we would cherish every moment together.

My marriage didn't turn out the way I prayed it would. A few years after we got married, trials came and so did my silence. No way was I going to talk about my problems; no way was I going to give up. I decided to stand for my marriage, to stand for my home. I had two wonderful boys – Christopher and Ethan – who needed the stability of a happy home. I was so blinded by my past hurt that I was willing to sacrifice my happiness to ensure that the image of what I thought life should be, remained. My marriage must work. That was my stance. But more than the image I had created in my mind, was the love I felt for my husband. I adored him and I really wanted my home to be the happy home it was supposed to be.

One day, I had to accept a bitter truth – it takes two to make a marriage work and since I was the only one fighting so hard, the burden became too much; the cracks started to become so visible and I just could not keep it up. I was so disappointed and ashamed. Once again, I had questions. Who could I tell? Where could I turn for advice and support? We were a young couple with no mentors or role models; we had no examples to follow. Simply put, we had no guidance whatsoever.

I believe marriage is God-ordained, but its success is a function of a successful partnership with God. We have a responsibility to do our part to make it as beautiful as it's meant to be. I know, in my heart, I did my part and continued to do so for many years until I realised that in trying to fight alone, I was hurting myself. I was a broken woman whose mental, physical, and emotional health was at stake. I decided to seek legal help and shortly after, the divorce was finalised. It was painful. Letting go was one of the hardest things I have ever had to do. After so many years of holding on and trusting God to restore my marriage, I had to accept the truth that it was finally over.

TURNING TRIALS INTO TRIUMPHS

We were married for 19 years so trust me when I say the relationship broke me as it broke down. I was exhausted and weary, and once more, I was alone again. Even though I had my two sons, I experienced a type of loneliness that happens even in a crowded room. I was alone with my thoughts and pains. No one gets married with the intention of getting divorced, especially someone like me who was so desperate for my family life to be stable. It was my dream for all of us to remain together.

I have come to learn from my experiences in life that God has a way of making something beautiful out of our trials and tribulations. The Bible tells us – in Isaiah 61 – that He gives beauty for ashes and I know this, not just as scripture, but as truth. I look at my life now and I cannot believe how much I have grown through grace. I can boldly say, I am not the same woman I used to be – God has transformed me and made me beautiful inside out.

I have achieved so much after the divorce because God lifted me and taught me the truths that I will share with you in the rest of this book. My life, truly, is an example that one can rise above challenges, and that, there can be a full life, after divorce. Yes, there is light at the end of the tunnel; even if it looks dark now, just keep walking and you will soon see the glow.

My purpose is to use my past challenges to encourage and motivate women that have shared some of my life's experiences or women who are going through other difficult circumstances. Regardless of what it is, I want to be there for you through the pages of this book. I have been able to impact so many lives through the social enterprise I founded in November 2012 – Women Empowering Projects. This was a vision God gave me, many years ago, when I was still going through my marital challenges. God showed me that He had a plan and a purpose for me.

At first, I was reluctant to launch out with the vision because I thought I didn't have anything to offer since I was still praying for restoration in my marriage. I was still hurting and broken myself, but I stepped out in faith and started reaching out to vulnerable women and in the process, God brought me healing and deliverance from my past pain and anguish. I didn't realise that when God sends you on a mission, it is not only for His glory but also, for your good. While I was doing His business, He was bringing such healing and deliverance to my own life. It has truly been amazing. As is said, "When you water others, you will be watered as well."

Regardless of what has happened in the past, I am still full of hope that my best is yet to come. I am expectant that God will do exceedingly abundantly above all I can ever ask or imagine. I have a positive expectation that whatever I am hoping for in life will surely come to pass. I refuse to allow my past determine my future and that of my children. My past has no hold over me anymore and I have been set free.

I invite you to journey with me through this book to find out how you too can turn your trials into triumphs. All I have written in this book are things that I still reflect on and apply today. I believe that we can never stop learning and each day, I am determined to continue to live the best version of me. Trials in life are not over because every day, something new comes my way. However, I have acquired the tools I need to cope with everyday life and I am so privileged to share them with you.

2

MINDSET MATTERS

*O**nce your mindset changes, everything on the outside will change along with it ~ Steve Maraboli*

My mindset was the first thing I had to address during those trying times of my life because I came to realise that how I saw myself, on the inside, would shape my reality. I pictured myself overcoming my challenges and coming out victorious. I knew I had to do whatever it took to make sure I had a positive mindset so I could see the good in my challenges.

We need to understand that our mindsets are mental attitudes that have taken shape based on our experiences in life, our environments, our education, and the ideas and beliefs we have absorbed from those people we have most interacted with in life. Our mindsets are responsible for how we interpret and react to what happens to and around us. A positive empowering mindset is needed to interpret challenges, setbacks, and criticisms in a way that is beneficial to us. Positive mindsets focus on the bright side of life and expect positive results. A positive person not only anticipates happiness, health, and success but also believes he or she can overcome any obstacles and difficulties. Never allow setbacks and disappointments affect your mindset because a positive mindset is required to bounce back from life's challenges.

HOW TO GET THE RIGHT MINDSET:

POSITIVE ATTITUDE

A positive attitude is required to maintain positive thinking when facing challenges. A positive attitude will help you cope more easily with the daily affairs of life. It brings optimism into your life and makes it easier to avoid worries and negative thinking. Having a positive attitude is a decision we need to make. I had to do this and today, I still have to make a decision to check my attitude when faced with challenges. I am not saying it is easy to maintain a positive attitude, but you need to be intentional about it. Don't allow your challenges to have a negative impact on your attitude; learn to forgive anyone that has wronged you by finding something positive in whatever has been done to you.

WAYS TO MAINTAIN A POSITIVE ATTITUDE

SMILE: Learn to smile in the face of adversity. Think of a happy memory and keep smiling about it; this will give you an instantaneous attitude boost. Apparently, smiling releases endorphins and serotonin, also known as the feel-good hormones. So, smile often in order to adopt a positive attitude from these chemicals in your body.

CHANGE YOUR THOUGHTS: Positive thoughts lead to positive attitudes while negative thoughts lead to negative attitudes. Anytime you find yourself focusing on negative thoughts, quickly pause and choose to think differently.

FOCUS ON THE GOOD: In order to have a positive attitude, you must focus on the good times; the good in others, the good in your life, and your achievements to date.

TURNING TRIALS INTO TRIUMPHS

VISUALISATION: When faced with challenges, keep a positive attitude by visualising yourself coming out victorious. Remember, the law of attraction says what you focus on will automatically come to fruition, so see yourself on the winning side of life.

UNDERSTAND THAT LIFE IS NOT EASY: I've come to understand that we don't have control over what happens to us. Know that life happens and be prepared for it. Not preparing for it will result in you having a negative attitude. Know that sometimes things won't be easy, and adopt the mental attitude that you have what it takes to deal with anything that life throws at you.

USE POSITIVE AFFIRMATIONS

Affirmations are proven methods of self-improvement because of their ability to rewire our brains. Much like exercise, they raise the level of feel-good hormones and push our brains to form new clusters of positive thought. I understand how setbacks and life's challenges can affect the way you feel about yourself. They can make you feel insecure, have low self-esteem, and also, affect your confidence to the extent that you lack the motivation to do the things you once had a passion for. I suffered most of these when my marriage broke down.

I can testify that there is so much power in declaring positive confessions to yourself in those trying times. This, I will say, was one of the tools I used to bounce back and regain my confidence. I wrote them out on a notepad and said them out loud every day. I'm still doing this today. This has led to me sending positive declarations to all the people on my mailing lists on Mondays and I've received a lot of positive feedback. The key is to repeat the affirmations to yourself each day so you flood your brain with the positive thoughts.

SOME OF MY AFFIRMATIONS

- All things are working together for my good.
- I am beautiful inside and out.
- God is restoring the years that were stolen from me.
- I am living life to the fullest.
- I have a prosperous mindset.
- I embrace every new season God has for me.
- The past has no power over me anymore.
- I am strong and courageous.
- I am in God's perfect timing in everything I do.
- I am secure in who I am and how I look.

STAY IN THE RIGHT ENVIRONMENT

Your environment plays a vital role in overcoming setbacks and challenges. It is easy to be positive and see light at the end of the tunnel in a positive environment. You need to be careful who you surround yourself with, in those trying periods. You do not need to be surrounded by negative people because if you are, trust me, it will be hard to move forward and bounce back from what you are going through. Choose your friends wisely and associate with people that will give you wise counsel. Also, be careful who you share your story with knowing that it is difficult to get advice from someone who hasn't been through a similar experience. Understand that not everyone is mature enough to give you advice. People you spend most of your time with will either influence you positively or negatively, so bid goodbye to anyone that is having a negative influence on you. If you find yourself in a relationship where you've been abused either physically, verbally, or emotionally, this is definitely a negative environment, which is not healthy for you. Please seek help and extricate yourself. Value your life enough not to subject yourself to an unhealthy environment.

EMBRACE DETERMINATION

Determination is a positive emotional feeling that involves persevering towards a difficult goal in spite of obstacles ~ Wikipedia.

I believe determination is a decision or the focus you need to get something done. I was determined not to allow my challenges affect me. However, I did not make this decision immediately, while going through the trials, but when I noticed how the challenges were affecting me emotionally, which in turn affected the quality of life I was living, I had to make a decision. I came to a crossroad where I had to make up my mind if I wanted the circumstances to break or make me. I decided to live my life to the fullest, regardless of the challenges being faced.

If I could do it, I believe you can too. You need to be determined not to give up on life in spite of your present circumstances. No matter how tough things are and how badly you want to give up, you need to keep on going. Sometimes, you may just want to let go when it seems like what you are going for is out of reach. At other times, you ask yourself if what you are trying to get is worth the great amount of effort you're putting in. But let me tell you this, the more pain and suffering you put into something, the better it will feel when you get it. Remember, determination is not giving up during difficult periods in life; determination is not letting go during difficult periods in life. It is falling flat on your face and getting back up.

Please apply this principle to any area of your life, whether it is starting a business, trusting God for a breakthrough in your relationship, or waiting to become a parent and I can assure you of results if you remain steadfast in your determination. I encourage you to never give up, but instead, remain hopeful.

LIVING A LIFE OF GRATITUDE

I have made gratitude my lifestyle by calling myself, Grateful Rachel. I did this because it is my belief that living a life of gratitude makes you happier and gives you a positive attitude to life in general. This allows you to see life's challenges differently; it makes you appreciate the good in your life as opposed to what is lacking. I remember, in September 2015, when I was about to sign the legal document of the divorce, I was so disheartened and wanted to give up on myself. However, I encouraged myself to take out a pen and paper to write what I had been able to achieve in life and what was working well for me. By the time I finished writing, I felt uplifted. This led me to throw the first Women Empowering Projects Gratitude Party in November 2015 and the outcome was totally awesome.

Thinking about who and what you are grateful for is important for the following reasons:

- It reminds you of the positive things in your life. It makes you happy about the people in your life, whether they are loved ones or just strangers you met who were kind to you in some ways.

- It reminds you of what is important. It's hard to complain about the little things when you give thanks that you and your children are alive and well. It will also be hard to get stressed out over paying bills when you are grateful for having a roof over your head.

- It turns bad things into good things. If you are having problems at work, be grateful that you have a job. Be grateful you have challenges, and that life isn't boring. Be grateful that you can learn from these challenges; be thankful, they make you a stronger person.

- It reminds you to appreciate others who God has placed in your life to make your journey bearable. Your family and friends are part of these people. It is important to say thank you to them for being there in times of need. From time to time, call or send an email, or even stop by to say hello and thank them. People like being appreciated for who they are and what they do, so just taking that minute to tell them why you are grateful to them, is important.

I came across this prayer of gratitude below and it has really blessed me.

BE THANKFUL

Be thankful that you don't already have everything you desire. If you did, what would there be to look forward to?

Be thankful when you don't know something, for it gives you the opportunity to learn.

Be thankful for the difficult times; during those times you grow.

Be thankful for your limitations because they give you opportunities for improvement.

Be thankful for each new challenge because it will build your strength and character.

Be thankful for your mistakes, they will teach you valuable lessons.

Be thankful when you're tired and weary because it means you've made a difference.

It is easy to be thankful for the good things.
A life of rich fulfilment comes to those who are also thankful for the setbacks.

GRATITUDE can turn negative into positive
Find a way to be thankful for your troubles
And they can become your blessings.
~ Author Unknown~

3

LOVING YOURSELF

*L**ove is the great miracle cure. Loving ourselves works miracles in our lives ~ Louise L. Hay*

Loving yourself, in spite of adversity, is one of the most important things you can do in order to achieve a satisfying and meaningful life filled with joy. If you love yourself so much you will find it easy enough to bounce back from challenges mainly because you place a higher value on yourself than on the challenges.

When setbacks occur and challenges come, there is a tendency to neglect our health because we allow depression set in, which results in us lacking the motivation to keep living life to the fullest. In the midst of all the adversity, you must make self-love a top priority. Many people fall into the trap of putting everyone else's needs – those of their children, spouses, and friends – before theirs and never taking a moment out for themselves. If you keep this up, you will soon drain your own tank and once this happens there will be nothing left to give. That's why it's so important to recharge, to take a breather, and put yourself first. Not doing so is a recipe for disaster. Remember, in order to love others and be loved in return, you need to first love yourself.

During those difficult times in my life, it took a while for me to master self-love. The feeling of rejection after the divorce wasn't helpful at all. I felt like a failure, which affected the way I perceived myself. My self-love tank was empty at the time. I had to gradually build myself up in order to overcome this feeling.

HOW TO SHOW YOURSELF LOVE

You must take care of your body. Many people turn to alcohol, drugs, smoking, and overeating to numb emotional pain. Though these might work in the short-term, over the long haul, it only serves to make your life worse instead of better.

Below are some things I did, which I will recommend you also do to shower yourself with love.

FITNESS

Those who know me can testify that I've taken my fitness level up a notch. Running, in particular, really helped me cope well during those trying times. It has been said that physical fitness allows you to perform daily activities, work well, and face stress or unexpected situations during moments of increased intensity.

I used food as a source of comfort when going through my marital challenge a few years ago, which resulted in me gaining unnecessary weight. I remember growing up to size 22 at a point, which is difficult to believe because of how I look today.

Physical fitness has lots of health benefits and I encourage you to identify an exercise you enjoy and be committed to doing it so you can improve your stamina and overall health. A good example is walking, which if done for just 20 minutes a day, will go a long way.

Regular exercise has been proven to:

- ❖ Reduce stress
- ❖ Boost self-esteem
- ❖ Strengthen the heart
- ❖ Get rid of anxiety and feelings of depression
- ❖ Improve sleep
- ❖ Increase energy levels
- ❖ Lower blood pressure
- ❖ Help reduce body fat

In addition to endorphins triggering positive feelings in the body, it has been proven that when you exercise, your body releases endorphins which interact with the receptors in your brain that reduce your perception to pain.

HEALTHY EATING

Another way of loving yourself is to make sure you embrace healthy eating habits. As earlier mentioned, I fell off the wagon when I was faced with challenges a few years ago. It is easy to cultivate bad eating habits when you are sad and feel hopeless. While food may numb the pain, it will not get rid of the challenges in the long run. Be intentional about what you put in your mouth and choose a healthy lifestyle. When at the supermarket, avoid going to the aisles where unhealthy foods are located and try not to go shopping when you are very hungry or when you are feeling low because it will be difficult to make healthy food choices at such times. Learn the benefits of each food type and eat them in moderation with an awareness that too much of even the healthy food choices will have negative after effects. There are guides online showing how much of what we eat should come from each food group to achieve a healthy balanced diet.

HEALTH CHECK UP

I believe that your health is your wealth. A health check is an examination of your current state of health, often carried out by your GP. Please make sure you undergo a variety of tests to ensure you are on the right track to good health. It has been proven that stress from everyday life releases toxins into our body. I want you to love yourself enough to carry out a health check at least once a year. Don't assume because you are not sick, you don't need to do a general check-up, remember prevention is better than cure. Some people have died untimely deaths because of negligence and ignorance. I also encourage you to take necessary supplements to boost your immunity.

DRESS WELL AND SHOW UP

I often say your appearance matters a lot. The way you dress says a lot about you, so much so that, when people see you for the first time your physical appearance will be impressed on their minds, possibly forever. I don't want my appearance to project that I have challenges in my life. I definitely did not pay attention to my dressing few years ago; I was too consumed with my challenges that I didn't pay much attention to myself. Looking at past pictures horrifies me because of the way I look in most of them. But I am not that girl anymore; I've decided to always look my best no matter what I face. I now take pride in how I look, not to impress anyone, but because I know the importance of loving myself. Make time for yourself and don't allow those setbacks and circumstances make you look older than you really are.

Get the right products for your face and create time to do your hair. Never look unkempt, as we don't want our children to hide us from their friends because they are too ashamed of our appearance. This is one thing I've decided not to take lightly anymore. During those difficult moments in my life, I made sure I looked my best regardless of what I was facing. We don't need plenty of money to look good, the trick is to know what sort of styles fit your body shape and wear what you are comfortable with. Shop when sales are on to avoid buying at full price. Try not to shop when you are feeling low so you don't become an emotional shopper because you will buy stuff you don't really need and you will overspend. I'm talking from experience when I would go shopping to relieve my mind of the situation at home and I would end up with a lot of stuff paid for with my credit card, which resulted in unnecessary debt. Don't allow your emotions control your spending but instead, be in control of your emotions.

PERSONAL DEVELOPMENT

We all have dreams and aspirations before setbacks, disappointments, and challenges set in. At such times, it is so easy to let go of our dreams, but I am grateful to God for the strength and determination I had when I was facing the marital challenge. I went back to university to train as a teacher after which I was able to set up a tutoring business and increase my income so that I could have financial freedom. It has been proven that some women stay in unhappy relationships mainly because they can't support themselves and their children financially and as a result, subject themselves to many years of torture in those relationships. I encourage you to improve your skill area so you are able to look after yourself when those unforeseen challenges surface. It's never too late to learn a new skill, if need be, for self-development. I know of a lady who has now gone back to university after a separation from her spouse. This has increased her self-esteem and boosted her confidence as well. Don't allow challenges to steal your dreams, but instead, use them as stepping-stones to greatness.

DETERMINE WHO YOU ARE

Never allow your circumstances define you. I battled a lot with the way I felt people would perceive me as a divorcee – I feared the stigma of being divorced. I was ashamed of the social status of divorcees and it was always a hurdle anytime I had to state my marital status. Also, being the only one amongst friends and family has been a struggle. I soon came to realise that my marital status didn't determine who I was as a person. I did not come to this world married and I will depart this world as I came when the time comes. My life purpose doesn't depend on my marital status either. My Maker fearfully and wonderfully made me, and He loves me so much, regardless. Thank God I'm now at peace with who I am

TURNING TRIALS INTO TRIUMPHS

and now I am living life to the fullest, as my past doesn't matter anymore.

4

A LIFE OF SIGNIFICANCE

What counts in life is not the mere fact that we have lived. It is what difference we have made to the lives of others that will determine the significance of the life we lead ~ Nelson Mandela.

I made a decision to live a significant life by looking for significance and finding it in everything I did, despite my circumstances. We can find value, positivity, and meaning in our day-to-day lives. I wanted to make my life count regardless of my challenges so I refused to allow my circumstances alter my purpose and destiny. I wanted to be a voice of hope to other women that have experienced or are still going to experience things similar to what I went through. In the midst of my challenges, still trusting God, and hoping that my marriage would be restored, I founded Women Empowering Projects with a vision to encourage, motivate, and empower women to make the most of their lives. I want women to be able to find purpose and fulfilment in life.

ADD VALUE TO OTHERS

Part of living a life of significance is adding value to others when we have the opportunity to boost their confidence, encourage their passions, and drive them to success. Something as simple as a smile or an opened door can add value to others around you. Be totally genuine in your actions to value people. Build positive relationships with people by beginning to acknowledge one good quality in them every time you have an opportunity. You are definitely adding value and making a great impact this way. To continue to value others, you must take time out to value yourself as well because if your cup is not full, you can't fill the cup of anyone around you. Refuel yourself every day with exercise, meditation, prayer, a good meal, and being grateful for life.

BE A BLESSING TO OTHERS

"Whoever brings blessing will be enriched, and one who waters will himself be watered" - Proverbs 11:25.

When faced with challenges, setbacks and disappointments, I will encourage you to take your eyes off your own situation and instead, set them on those around you. I'm not implying that this is easy to do, especially when your circumstances are not changing. However, I've learned that the best way to forget your own problems is to help someone else with theirs. Bring yourself to notice the need of those God has set in your path and find ways to meet their needs. I want to become someone's miracle by showing God's love and mercy everywhere I go. You can use your story to be a light in the place of darkness to others. I believe there's good in every darkness, but you have to be willing to see the good in your circumstances.

WAYS TO BE A BLESSING TO OTHERS

1) Just listen: Sometimes, all people need is for you to listen to them; they just need someone to talk to and confide in. A lot of people are lonely and feel hopeless. I don't want to be too consumed with my own challenges that I cannot notice

such people that God has sent my way. Make yourself available and approachable so people find it easy to want to talk to you. I am grateful for the opportunity God has given me to be able to do this through Women Empowering Projects and the 'Shine from Within' program that I launched in April 2017. I'm always praying for God to give me good listening skills so, this way, I can be a blessing.

2) Encouragement: You can be a blessing to people by simply encouraging others to keep on keeping on in the midst of their challenges. Just saying to someone, "It's going to be alright," can go a long way. I benefited from people taking time out to encourage me when I was at a crossroad and felt like giving up on myself during those difficult times in my life. Still, having people who are encouraging me to date is helping me carry on with life.

3) Give: Giving makes us more blessed than we would be if we were only receivers. If you have the means to give financially to someone in a financial crisis, please go ahead and do it. Apart from giving financially, fundraising and donating new or used goods can go a long way

as well, as others will appreciate those items you don't find useful anymore. I am again grateful for the opportunity to do charity runs to raise funds for five different organisations. It gives me so much satisfaction to be able to make a difference in the lives of others in my own little way. This happened in August 2016 when I thought to myself that since I enjoy running, I might as well start entering races to raise funds for different charities. That's where the journey began. The discipline, as well as the perseverance and consistency in running, have really helped my mental and physical wellbeing. Don't allow the size of your gift keep you from giving; the most important thing is that you give from your heart. I also had the privilege to organise two Charity Balls in July 2016 and 2017 and raised a substantial amount for four different charities based in the UK and in Africa. This is now going to be a yearly event to continue raising funds for different organisations.

4) Volunteer: This is another way you can be a blessing to your community. There are so many organisations that need people to volunteer their time and expertise. Homeless shelters, orphanages, care homes, and food banks can all

use a helping hand. Just an hour or two of your time will have an impact on someone for a lifetime. I am so blessed to be in a church where this form of giving is recognised greatly.

GET OUT OF YOUR COMFORT ZONE

A comfort zone is a psychological state in which things feel familiar to a person and they are at ease and in control of their environment and experience low level of anxiety and stress ~ Wikipedia.

Living a life of significance will definitely require you leaving your comfort zone. I had to leave my comfort zone, a year ago, to start my motivational messages on Facebook. Part of leaving my comfort zone is me writing this book. I am not naturally gifted to write, but I was able to push through knowing I have a story that can bless others. I've come to realise that the more time we spend outside our comfort zones, the more we achieve and when we achieve, it spurs us on to push our comfort zones further and achieve even more. Being slightly uncomfortable, whether or not by choice, can push us to achieve goals we never thought we could.

Stepping out of your comfort zone will help you embrace change, try new things, achieve your goals, meet new people, push your limits, feel motivated, aim higher, and help define you as a person. I wasn't aware how strong I was until I was faced with the challenges. The strength to persevere came from somewhere and I can testify that my life is richer and better and I'm hopeful that the best is yet to come.

DON'T BE IDLE

Occupy yourself with different tasks so you don't become idle. Too much time on your hands can cause unnecessary and unhealthy thought processes to begin. If you are preoccupied, there will not be time for you to get depressed. Think of a new hobby to do or you can enrol at a local college to learn a new skill.

5

NAVIGATING DIFFERENT SEASONS OF LIFE

To everything, there is a season,

A time for every purpose under heaven:

A time to be born, and a time to die;

A time to plant, and a time to pluck what is planted;

A time to kill, and a time to heal;

A time to break down, and a time to build up;

A time to weep, and a time to laugh;

A time to mourn, and a time to dance;

A time to cast away stones, and a time to gather stones;

A time to embrace, and a time to refrain from embracing;

A time to gain, and a time to lose;

A time to keep, and a time to throw away;

A time to tear, and a time sew;

A time to keep silence, and a time to speak;

A time to love, and a time to hate;

A time of war, and a time of peace. ~ Ecclesiastes 3:1-8

One thing I can honestly say is that seasons of life are temporary, which means none of the challenges in our lives will last forever. I want you to rest assured in the knowledge that your unfortunate circumstances are bound to change. I have matured and grown as a person through my different seasons and I have now learnt to embrace every season I find myself in. Seasons of life are there to teach us lessons about ourselves, others, and about life. They are there to help us grow emotionally, physically, and socially, and also, to harden our souls and strengthen our emotional resilience in the face of adversity and opportunity.

We must understand the seasons. If we do not understand that there are seasons in life, we may draw wrong conclusions about what is happening in our lives. God has a plan and purpose to make your life beautiful, regardless of your circumstances. In tough times where health, money, friends, and marriages are not looking good, we may wonder what is going on, but God makes us beautiful through all the trials and circumstances of life. This is exactly what God has done in my own life and I am a living proof of this.

Hanging on to a previous season instead of embracing the current season can be detrimental to your progress. Never try to push something that is not meant to be in the wrong season. Forget what lies behind and push forward to what lies ahead.

WHAT TO KNOW ABOUT SEASONS

1) Change of seasons is not an indication that you are good or bad. The fact that a bad thing happens to you does not mean you are a bad person; understand that, bad things happen to good people too. I always tell people that life happens and knowing this will help you bounce back from any setbacks and disappointments.

2) Don't allow the season you are in define you as a person. Be careful not to change your beliefs and values because of your current season. Never

make a life-changing decision based on how you feel in that season, bearing in mind that your feelings are just temporary emotions that will not last forever.

3) Learn to be consistent in every season. Consistency is the key to achieving anything you set your heart on. Don't allow seasons shift your focus from achieving your dreams. Do the work that the season you are in requires. Like farmers, there are times for planting, resting, watering, and harvesting. A lot of preparatory work is required in order to reap a great harvest.

4) Learn from every season. There are lessons to be learnt in every season that you are in. I've learnt so much, over the years, at different seasons. I've learnt to be patient, to endure, and persevere. I believe the lessons learnt from every season will be useful to counsel any friends or acquaintances going through similar seasons. Whatever you learnt in your dark season can be used to encourage others who may face the same kinds of things you faced in the future.

5) Guard your heart in every season. Our heart condition greatly influences the course and direction of our lives. We can't control what

happens around us, but we can control what happens inside us. You have no control over how people treat you, but you can control how you respond to them. Don't give anybody or any situation the power to mess around with your heart.

PEOPLE COME AND GO

I am a firm believer that everything happens for a reason. People come to our lives for different reasons and at different seasons. I believe everyone that comes into your life is a piece of the puzzle. And once all the pieces have been placed together, the puzzle is complete, thus fulfilling your journey. Understand that not everyone that comes to your life is there to stay forever. My ex-husband came to my life for those 19 years and his departure was definitely difficult to comprehend, but his time was up and the grace of God has kept me and the boys ever since. Friends come and go, and life goes on. People will come into your life for a reason, a season, or a lifetime. The following poem sheds more light on this:

REASON, SEASON, OR LIFETIME

People come into your life for a reason, a season or a lifetime.

When you figure out which one it is,

You will know what to do for each person.

When someone is in your life for a REASON,

It is usually to meet a need you have expressed.

They have come to assist you through a difficulty;

To provide you guidance and support;

To aid you physically, emotionally, or spiritually.

They may seem like a godsend, and they are.

They are there for the reason you need them to be.

Then, without any wrongdoing on your part or at an inconvenient time,

This person will say or do something to bring the relationship to an end.

Sometimes they die. Sometimes they walk away.

Sometimes they act up and force you to take a stand.

What we must realize is that our need has been met, our desire fulfilled; their work is done.

TURNING TRIALS INTO TRIUMPHS

The prayer you sent up has been answered and now it is time to move on.

Some people come into your life for a SEASON,

Because your turn has come to share, grow, or learn.

They bring you an experience of peace or make you laugh.

They may teach you something you have never done.

They usually give you an unbelievable amount of joy.

Believe it. It is real. But only for a season.

LIFETIME relationships teach you lifetime lessons;

Things you must build upon in order to have a solid emotional foundation.

Your job is to accept the lesson, love the person,

And put what you have learned to use in all other relationships and areas of your life.

It is said that love is blind but friendship is clairvoyant.

~Unknown Author

SEASON OF WAITING

I can still remember, vividly, my season of waiting for a turnaround in my marriage and for God to heal my broken heart. It was difficult and painful; not knowing whether or not the breakthrough would happen and how long it would take.

One thing is clear, nobody enjoys waiting for anything. It can be very frustrating and a greater dose of patience is needed at this very crucial season in life. Whereas God does some of His best work in us during the waiting seasons of life, I've come to realise that our timing isn't God's timing, but the one thing I know is that His timing is always best. When waiting for God, we often don't understand that His silence, His seeming non-responsiveness is because He has our best interests at heart. Waiting is hard work and it tests our faith. It's especially difficult when there is no guarantee that our waiting will end in this lifetime, but we must continue to be hopeful and know that God cares. Waiting for God to speak and direct us should be a way of life. A period of waiting serves as a time of preparation. If God were to answer us right away, many of us would be ill-prepared to handle the situation. Beyond the ability to wait, as important as it is, how we wait really matters. We must maintain a good attitude at this time and not lose focus or hope.

In my own experience, it's in this season of waiting and being still before God while pouring my heart out before him, that He does some of His greatest work for me. It's in the quietness of the desert that God can restore my hope and vision and deepen my character. It's in waiting that I get to know God's heart more intimately and finally begin to realise He is in my life.

Whatever you might be waiting for in life, I want you to know that the Faithful One who not only knows and loves us but also has a plan and purpose for each of us, will come through for you at His own appointed time. Remember that a delay is not a denial. When you think God is saying "No," He may just be saying, "Not yet." While you are waiting, God is working; don't think that the season of waiting means God has stopped working. He's just taking you through that season because He's using the time to work in your circumstances for your good.

6

SUPPORT SYSTEM

Sometimes, we need someone to simply be there. Not to fix anything in particular, but just to let us feel that we are cared for and supported.

When things aren't going well or we're just not feeling great, we all need support and encouragement. Having the right support system during my marital breakdown contributed a great deal to my success in navigating the challenges. For those who try to do it alone, it can be a difficult uphill battle. On the other hand, much wisdom, experience, and insight can be gained from friends, family, or colleagues who have been there and have learnt what it takes to prevail. It is important not to try to deal with challenges entirely on your own.

Building and maintaining a strong support system is a vital part of your self-care plan.

HOW DOES A SUPPORT SYSTEM HELP

1) Improved physical and emotional health: Support systems have been proven to be beneficial for maintaining physical and mental health by helping to protect against depressive conditions.

2) Accountability: Being accountable to someone else has been shown to be a key factor in making successful lifestyle changes. Accountability works best when reciprocated; in addition to reporting your progress to someone else, allow that person to be accountable to you as well.

3) Better problem solving: Social support groups can help you work out problems and relieve stress. Regardless of what you are experiencing, chances are others are dealing with similar issues and may be able to provide you with useful strategies.

4) Enhanced brain fitness: Even if you are not looking for a supportive network to help you

resolve specific issues, the interaction is still important for keeping your brain fit. Look for opportunities to stay engaged with people. Consider joining or increasing your involvement in recreational, leisure, or faith-based groups formed around activities you enjoy. Also, explore attending networking meetings where you have the opportunity to meet different people from different walks of life; such interactions will help you stay mentally sharp.

COUNSELLING

I was advised to go for counselling by a friend when I was stuck and confused about what step to take during the marital challenge. I must say it was very helpful to talk to someone who had been trained to offer me the support that was needed at that time. The counselling sessions shed a lot more light on my situation, so I will highly recommend this to people.

Having someone to talk to who is there specifically to listen to you talk about your feelings, is an invaluable benefit to many people. Often, people take solace in talking to friends and family, but for many people, this can actually be a barrier to openly and honestly discussing their issues. Many people feel more comfortable talking to a trained professional who is, essentially, a stranger and who can, therefore, listen to them without judgement. They are also experienced in dealing with and talking about almost any subject, so there's nothing you need to feel too embarrassed or ashamed to talk about.

Sharing and unloading your emotions through counselling and talking means you can get on with the rest of your life, making it easier to cope. When you have some weight on your mind, knowing you can rely on someone to listen to your problems, frees you from worrying about them all the time. This means you can focus on living your life again.

Speaking aloud and verbalising your thoughts and emotions, lets you see them from a new perspective, instead of just in your own mind. Saying them to another person also makes you consider what their view is, meaning you can gain new ways of thinking about your problems by simply letting them out. Similarly, letting things out that you've been keeping in can be a cathartic experience, purging you of pent-up emotions, as many people find they are relieved of thoughts or feelings that they'd bottled up. Such a release often feels like a weight off your mind and allows people to begin to let go of feelings they've been holding on to.

As we can be too busy with our day-to-day schedule, this means we can rarely afford the time to sit and process feelings of sadness, disappointment, remorse, or grief. Counselling means you simply dedicate some time to facing or confronting your issues. When you have an appointment with another person, you're committed to them for that period of time, meaning you can't put off or run away from facing your feelings. Equally, you're less likely to be distracted while you are facing those feelings.

Counselling can help you understand yourself better and the way you think, which will, ultimately, help you develop a clearer understanding of your problems. The more armed with information you are, the easier it gradually becomes to navigate your way through any difficulties you are facing so that you can, eventually, come out on the other side feeling more positive. Counselling can also help you better understand other people's points of view, which can shed light on the way you interpret words or actions.

While counsellors may not give you concrete advice or a checklist of things to do to feel better, they will help you uncover your own insight and understanding of your problems, providing you with the tools which will help you to resolve them on your own. Counselling is a journey, and it takes time and consistency to work effectively, because of this, many people opt for regular counselling sessions to make the most of the process.

7

FORGIVENESS

To forgive is to set a prisoner free and discover that the prisoner was you ~ Lewis B. Smedes

In order to bounce back from the past, you must learn to forgive whoever has offended you. We must realise that forgiveness is for our own growth and happiness. When we hold on to hurt, pain, resentment, and anger, it harms us more than it harms the offender. Forgiveness lets us regain our personal power. Our anger, regret, hatred, or resentment towards someone means we are surrendering our power to that person. Mahatma Gandhi said, "Forgiving is an attribute of the strong, the weak can never forgive." Forgiveness puts you at peace and gives you an upper hand. Forgiveness is not accepting the bad done to you; it involves loving the person who gives pain. It removes the bitterness from deep within your heart and life. You should forgive, but never accept the lesson from the pain.

One thing I've realised is that forgiveness is a journey and a process; it will take a big effort on your part to forgive and let go completely. I must confess it wasn't easy for me after my break up, but I had to trust God to move past the hurt and the disappointment. As a Christian, forgiveness is one of the most important parts of the scripture. To walk with our heavenly Father, we must learn to forgive others, but the problem with forgiveness is that it is hard to do. When a person hurts us, we do not want to turn around and say, "I forgive you," because most likely at that moment, we are not ready to forgive them in our hearts. True forgiveness must come from your heart that is why it is important to ask God for help so that He may soften your heart.

When someone hurts us, we want vengeance and we want them to know our pain. This is when not forgiving someone leads to sin. For me, when I finally did forgive after my marital breakup, it was as if a weight had lifted off my heart.

There are times when it is not possible to forget something that has been done to you. Forgiveness does not mean it will instantly fix the friendship or relationship with the other person. What it does mean is you have come to terms with the occurrence and made your peace with what was done. God will always be there to help us through hard times and if we rely completely on Him, He will help us overcome hardships. God forgave our sins with the biggest sacrifice of all, so we should be able to forgive others and sacrifice our own pride.

A research called the Stanford Forgiveness Project has shown that learning to forgive lessens the amount of hurt, anger, stress, and depression that people experience. People who forgive also become more hopeful, optimistic, and compassionate and also have enhanced conflict resolution skills. This research also found that people who forgive report significantly fewer physical symptoms of stress such as backache, muscle tension, dizziness, headaches, and upset stomachs. The act of forgiveness also increases energy and overall wellbeing.

HOW TO FORGIVE

- Acknowledge the pain you feel and recognise who is responsible for it.

- Express your emotions in healthy ways.

- Find new ways to get your needs met in the future.

- Release any expectations you have of righting the wrong that was done to you.

- Acknowledge that what happened really happened, instead of wishing it were different.

- Release the unhealthy attachment you previously maintained concerning how the other person behaves.

LEAVE THE PAST BEHIND

Sometimes, we allow ourselves to remain in the past, as we are afraid to live in the present not knowing that, for every day we remain trapped in the past, countless amazing opportunities pass us by. It is so easy to allow unresolved past issues and regrets impact heavily on the present moments. Wishing we had done things differently and not gotten involved with certain people or frustration and anger surrounding other people's behaviour towards us, can all lead to wallowing in resentment and pain.

HOW TO OVERCOME THE PAST

1) Accept the past: Fully acknowledge that the past cannot be changed. We can't turn back the hands of the clock however much we would like to. What we can change, though, is how we view it now and how we allow it to still control our daily thoughts and emotions.

2) Confront the past: Try to find and use whatever means possible to confront the past. If it is too traumatic to do alone, find a counsellor or professional to help. Until we fully open our eyes to the reality of the past and the circumstances surrounding it, we will be unable to ever fully understand it and set ourselves free.

3) Be aware of your thoughts: Whenever you recognise that your mind is wandering, rein in your thoughts. The less you think about things, the less power the thoughts will have over you. Remember thoughts lead to emotions, which

will then grow. Don't allow your energy to be wasted on negative thinking as this can cause you to experience pain from one single thought.

4) Forgive yourself: Understand that we all make mistakes, as no one is perfect. Learn and grow from whatever has happened. Take any positives from the experience that you can and leave the negatives where they belong.

5) Forgive others: Forgiving others will do you more good than it will do them. Release the anger and pain surrounding whatever has happened in the past. As soon as you learn to let go and forgive, the weight will immediately lift from your shoulders.

6) Start afresh: Take positive steps to remove all the old habits and routines and create a new existence, a happier one, with only healthy and loving thoughts for yourself. Take up new hobbies; fill your time so you have no time for idle thoughts about what no longer matters.

As soon as we move away from negativity, we instantly open ourselves up to the opportunity of attracting positivity. We attract exactly what we put out. Happiness attracts happiness and true love attracts true love. Until we move from a place of hurt and anger, we will continually attract more pain and anger into our lives.

Everything that has happened before is a preparation for what our future holds. They make us wiser, stronger, and more prepared for whatever is coming our way.

"When one door closes, another opens; but we often look so long and so regretfully upon the closed door that we do not see the one which has opened for us." ~ Alexander Graham Bell

HEALING FROM REJECTION

The pain of rejection has enveloped me for many years. I felt rejected for being abandoned as a child by my parents and from my ex-husband. My heart was empty and lonely for years and I cried out for love and acceptance. Rejection is a wound that must be healed for lasting freedom, life, and joy.

I had to go through the process of healing from rejection, recently, in order to break free from some of the unhealthy fruits rejection has caused in my life. It was difficult to realise the damage rejection has caused me. I discovered that if we receive rejection, our soul is affected but our human spirit is starved and therefore, is unable to sustain healthy life as it should. Roots of rejection can go down deep, causing a host of emotional challenges and behaviour that can surface later in life. The negative emotion of rejection can fuel insecurities and low self-esteem.

In order to deal with the pain of rejection and other painful emotions, we must have the courage to ask God and to look within. If we deny having deeper issues, we delay our deliverance. Looking within may require us to face some tough issues, but as we expose and uncover them, we allow God to do His work in us. This was exactly what I had to do to be set free from the pain of rejection.

The following verse in Psalms really puts the light on how we can be freed from the devastating effects of rejection:

When my father and my mother forsake me, then the LORD will take me up. Psalms 27:10

Knowing that you are accepted, loved, and appreciated by God will also help you move past the pain of rejection. Base your identity on what the Word of God says about you. We can become immune from the wounds of rejection as long as we are not basing our identity on what has happened to us in the past or what people think of us.

Finally, forgiving that person who has rejected us is a vital step in the healing process.

There is more to understand about this topic of healing from rejection. I will advise you to seek further help if you are suffering from this devastating pain, just like I did. Healing from any emotional pain is an ongoing process so please, make sure you give yourself enough time to overcome the pain from the past.

8

SINGLE PARENTING

Being a single parent is not a life full of struggles, but a journey for the strong ~ Meg Lowery

I am celebrating my older son's 19th birthday as I write this chapter of the book. Observing the very considerate, caring, gentle, and compassionate man he has become, as well as his heart for God, gladdens my heart. I am so thankful to God for the strength and wisdom He has given me to bring up my boys throughout the marital challenges. It hasn't been easy doing the job of both parents, but I know it wouldn't have been possible without God's help. I remember thinking I don't want my boys to grow up in a home with a single parent because I still recalled how I was affected by growing up without my own parents. Nothing in the world can be likened to a mother's love for her children; she wants the best for them and wants to protect them from anything that will negatively impact their future. As a mother, you will do whatever it takes to be there for them. The love I have for my boys kept me going during those trying times and I depended on God's grace every day to carry out my motherly duties.

Being the only parent responsible for every aspect of your children's lives is not an easy task. From choosing the right school for them and taking them to various activities to meeting their day-to-day needs as well. Being a single parent can result in added pressure, stress, and fatigue and if you are too tired or distracted to be emotionally supportive or consistently discipline your children, behavioural problems may arise. But, regardless of what research has shown in a single-parent family, your children can and will turn out well as I am a living testimony of this. So, be encouraged if you find yourself in this situation because it is not the end of the world as life goes on. Being in the position to offer protection, affection, and direction, which are the three things I believe children need, will help you give them all they require to thrive in life in spite of being raised by a single parent.

HOW TO MANAGE AS A SINGLE PARENT

- Build a support system: I know you want whatever it takes to go the distance alone, but you don't have to do that. Having a support system you can count on is absolutely vital, not just to survive the single parenthood, but to maintain your sense of self at the same time. Let the people in your life right now who care about you and your child(ren) become a source of support when you need it. You can also join an online single parents group for support.

- Create a routine: Having a regular routine will make life easier for you and the children. If this is not in place already, my advice is to quickly do so. If you have done this already, ask yourself where there might be room for developing even more regular routines around the things that you need to tackle every day. Things like making sure homework is done, preparation for school the following day, uniforms are washed and ironed, and the homework diary is signed. The children should also know things to do in the morning and evening.

- Ask for help: I know this is one of the hardest things to do, especially when you are used to being on your own. Don't be a superwoman; there is nothing wrong with asking for help. Asking for help doesn't mean you are weak and incapable of doing things, but it will give you a break when you need it. Also, find out the help that is available to you from the government; I believe in utilising every little help I can get. For example, I got my council tax reduced after my divorce as there was now one less adult in the house. You can get a lot of information from your local Citizen Advise Bureau.

- Develop ground rules: Establishing a clearly defined set of house rules makes it easier for your children to align their behaviour with your expectations. Start by sitting down with the children and developing a set of rules you are willing to abide by. Avoid coming up with a long, complicated set of rules, but instead, keep them simple and positive. Also, it should let your kids know what you expect of them at all times. Refer to the list of rules often as you work to shape your children's behaviour and decision making, with the goal of guiding them toward eventually making their own positive choices in life.

- Build strong relationships with your children: I consider myself blessed as I have been able to build a strong relationship with my boys, especially with my older son, Christopher, as he was more aware of the situation of things at home during the challenges. I opened up to him and explained what was happening so it didn't come as a total shock to him when the divorce finally came through. I must say I really struggled to bring myself to tell Ethan, my younger son, but I prayed for wisdom and help from God, and also to know the appropriate time to tell him. It eventually wasn't as bad as I thought it would be. God used that situation to bring me closer to my boys, and now, they are able to open up to me when they need to. We must know that our relationship with our children is one of the biggest influences on their behaviour and choices. Please do what it takes to keep your relationship close and strong. You don't necessarily have to be their best friend, but let them know they can tell you anything that is bothering them by being approachable. And when they do, listen to them without anger and judgement otherwise they will bottle up their thoughts, feelings, and emotions, or seek a listening ear elsewhere.

- Get mentors: This, I believe, is very important. The children will benefit from having someone they are looking up to. Knowing there are other adults who value them and care about their wellbeing can be a powerful force to help them develop positive self-esteem. Let them develop connections with other adult figures you trust. I am grateful that the boys have been able to make these connections with some of the amazing people in my spheres and at church.

- Set a positive example: Our children are observing and learning from us so it is important to make sure our lifestyle is worthy of emulation by our children. Let them learn determination and endurance by not giving up in time of adversity. It's paramount to maintain a positive attitude as well.

- Learn to say no: Don't allow the guilt of the situation at home force you to say yes to things you are meant to say no to. Children know when you are vulnerable and they might want to use this to manipulate you by asking for things they wouldn't normally ask for in the past.

- Set goals for yourself: Consider where you want to be one year from now, both personally and professionally. Write those goals down in a journal or share them with a friend who's willing to hold you accountable for taking steps toward making those dreams a reality. Don't let single parenting be an excuse for not achieving your dreams. Use this situation to your advantage; you can even use this to spur your children on by using your success to encourage them to attain great heights in life regardless of any challenges they face.

- Make time for fun: Create the time to have fun together as a family and just enjoy your kids. This will also help with building a strong relationship with the children.

- Take care of yourself: Understand that taking care of yourself is not selfish. You must find the strength to take good care of yourself during challenges and setbacks, especially when you have children that are dependent on you. I often tell people that you can't give what you don't have. Part of loving yourself is looking after yourself. When you take the time out to do the things you enjoy, you will come back home refreshed and enthusiastic enough to carry on, thus creating a positive environment conducive for the whole family.

- Live within your means: I know you might struggle financially at some point, that's why it's important to live within your means. Only buy what you can afford for the children at the moment and don't get into the practice of living on credit cards. Learn to make wise financial decisions so you can live comfortably with what you have coming in, bearing in mind that the season will not last forever.

- Don't feel guilty: It can happen that you feel guilty for not staying in the relationship for the sake of your children; I felt this way for a while. One thing I can say is that it is not healthy to force yourself to be in a relationship because of the kids only. If you know there's no more future for the two of you and your wellbeing is at stake, I will urge you to seek help and see whether or not the relationship can be restored. The truth is, no one gets married with the end of the marriage as his/her goal, but life happens and people change along the way. If you know you've given your best and the situation is still not changing, then there's no room for guilt. However, not giving your all to make things work is what I don't reckon with. As a single parent, don't allow guilt get in the way of meeting your children's physical and emotional needs. It is important to deal with your feelings in ways that are healthy for your family. Speak with a professional if the guilt you feel is getting in the way of living your life.

- Allow yourself time to heal: Going through a separation or divorce is not easy at all. You will need time to heal and this timescale will vary from one individual to the next. The pain will always be there, but you must find a coping mechanism for the sake of your emotional wellbeing. You have to be well enough to be there for your children when they need you. Spending time writing in a journal, going for a walk, or sharing your emotions with a friend will help to accelerate your healing process.

- Be civil with your ex: For the sake of the children, try to find a common ground with your ex if he's still willing to be involved in the lives of the children. If this is the case, it can lighten the burden a bit. Pray for the grace to do this if you are finding it difficult to accommodate him in the lives of the children. Put the past behind, as I mentioned in an earlier chapter, and be a better person.

9

MAINTAINING FAITH DURING CHALLENGES

Faith is not about everything turning out okay. Faith is about being okay no matter how things turn out ~ Annetta Powell

HAVE FAITH IN GOD

Faith is the confident assurance that something we want is going to happen. It is the certainty that what we hope for is waiting for us, even though we cannot see it up ahead. (Hebrew 11:1)

I know how difficult it is, not seeing any changes in those circumstances after you've prayed and made specific requests regarding the situation, hoping and trusting God that things will turn around for good, yet it feels like God is not willing to answer your prayer and bring you the relief you need. I want to encourage you to take heart and patiently wait for His perfect timing. Make a decision to believe that God's promises are true for everything is possible to the one who believes.

Express the confidence of faith by boldly declaring specific promises related to your situation and as you do, you will find that you have the peace and quiet assurance that God is at work in the situation, even though you might not see any outward changes yet.

When we go through tough times, the most important thing for us is to keep our faith in God, so continue to stand in faith until you see answers to your prayers.

We all face different challenges and situations in life; you might even be going through a season of difficulty in your life right now. Whatever it is, you can have the determination to see things through as you find your strength in God. When you are experiencing difficulties, the first place to deal with the issues is with yourself. Your attitude in challenging times could determine the outcome. While you might not be able to change the circumstances, you can certainly cooperate with God to change you.

No matter how bad the situation you are facing is, you can experience God's love, which nothing can separate you from. You have reason to shout even in your dark place, for you have the love of God and His word that all things are possible with Him.

TIMELY TRAINING

Do you know that God has a plan and a purpose for your life? Before your existence, in history, God appointed your days before one of them came to be (Psalm 139:16). How amazing and all-knowing our God is!

Despite what people, circumstances, or your thoughts attempt to tell you, remember God knew what He was doing when He divinely ordered your steps as you endured those challenges, sad times, disappointments, and setbacks. Your collective life experiences are working together for your good and training you for the plans, purposes, and will of God. As we journey through life as children of the Covenant, trusting God is absolutely paramount in our lives, although we might not understand all of the puzzle pieces until later in life.

But when we trust God, knowing that He loves us and will never leave nor forsake us, we are empowered to faithfully believe that His training is for where He is taking us. The training God has you going through is timely and purposeful. Your training is strengthening you for where God has ordained you to go. No matter what, remember obedience and faith are God's ways to the top.

BE GROUNDED IN GOD'S WORD

The change will come in you and in your life as you meditate on God's word. The word of God has been my anchor during the challenging periods in my life; I held on to all His promises regarding my circumstances. I was able to find God's promises that speak to my situation and say them back to myself day and night.

Allow God's Word to change you; you can only reap the full benefits of God's words as you apply them to your life. When this happens, there will be a change in your focus, and you will become more sensitive to what God's Word is saying about the circumstances you are facing.

SPEND TIME IN PRAYER

Prayer is communication with God. It is where you fellowship with Him and build a relationship. God encourages us to ask for the things we need. When faced with different challenges, spend time in prayer and ask Him to supply specific needs as He promises in His Word. In those trying times in my life, one of my many prayers was for God to supply me with the grace I needed to pull through each day, as I believe you need different graces every day to handle the circumstances you are facing. Every day is a new day and your emotions change daily as well.

- Ask God for what you need in Jesus' name.

- Pray in faith. Believe that whatever you ask for, based on the promises in His Word, you have received.

- Make sure you do not harbour unforgiveness in your heart, as this can hinder your faith and stop you from receiving what God has for you.

- Pray in the spirit if you can. The Holy Spirit helps you pray the perfect will of God concerning you and the situation you are going through.

RENEW YOUR MIND

"Do not conform to the pattern of this world, but be transformed by the renewing of your mind. Then you will be able to test and approve what God's will is – His good, pleasing and perfect will." (Romans 12:2).

Our thinking influences how we feel and behave. The above verse instructs us to constantly renew our minds. Your mindset could cause your life to be out of line with God's perfect will for you.

When you face challenging situations, you find that you become more focused on them. When this happens, your thinking begins to be shaped by the situations you are now focused on, which might result in thought patterns that are not in line with God's Word. You must consciously make the effort to focus on what God's Word says about you and your situation, and as you continue to do this, you will get God's perspective on the situation you are facing. Then, you will find that it is not a hopeless situation, for God is in the midst of it changing you, and ultimately, your circumstances. Soon you will see God using what was meant for evil to bless your life and the lives of others.

PRAISE AND THANKSGIVING

"Give thanks in all circumstances; for this is the will of God for you." (1 Thessalonians 5:18)

God desires that you give Him thanks and praise, in good times as well as in difficult situations. God never changes and His blessings are available in every situation you find yourself. When you take out time to praise, you are acknowledging His goodness in all seasons.

Praising God in the difficult times doesn't minimise or deny the heaviness of your heart, but it redirects your focus on who God is. He never changes and He promised never to leave or abandon His children, so we can count on His presence, even when our emotions can't confirm it; He is near to the broken-hearted.

I remember, there have been times when I thought, "I'll never be encouraged," but as soon as I began to remind myself of His mercy and goodness, praises burst out of my mouth immediately. It doesn't mean that those problems will suddenly disappear when this happens, but it does mean that my face will brighten again and the weight of the burden will lessen. Then, I'll be able to experience the joy of the Lord in the midst of life's storms and challenges.

When we think of praise, it may help to note that this includes Thanksgiving, speaking well of God, confessing faith, and an array of adoring expressions. The enemy is aware that as long as we wait for everything to line up before we praise the Lord, we'll stay stuck a lot longer than we need to be. We can have thankful hearts towards God even when we do not feel thankful for the circumstances. We can grieve and still be thankful. We can hurt and still be thankful. We can be angry at the sin and still be thankful towards God. That is what the Bible calls a sacrifice of praise. Giving thanks to God keeps our hearts in right relationship with Him and saves us from a host of harmful emotions and attitudes that will rob us of the peace God wants us to experience in life.

CHURCH COMMUNITY

It is important to be in a faith-filled church where you are being fed the Word of God so you can grow spiritually. It must be a church that can meet the needs of your children as well because you want to be where your children can develop their own relationship with God and have the opportunity to serve in their own capacity. During my marital challenge, I had to think of my boys' spirituality and because of this, I knew I had to find a local church that would nurture their faith in God. God led us to the church we are part of now and I am so thankful that the boys enjoy going to church and my older son is now one of the youth leaders and a role model for the younger one.

The church is sometimes called a fellowship; it is a network of relationships and we all need to give and receive fellowship. We all need to give and receive love. Fellowship means sharing lives and emotions, bearing one another's burdens, encouraging one another and helping people who have needs. This is the type of fellowship you need during trying times in your life so make sure you and your children, if you have any, are part of a church that can offer this.

10

EMOTIONAL WELL-BEING

Written by Dr Titi Osoba

The Bible declares that "the strong spirit of a man sustains him in bodily pain or trouble" Proverbs 18:14 [Amplified Bible, Classic Edition]. I also believe that the state of one's mind or emotions also determines how we respond in a time of crisis or adversity. The Bible says in 3 John: 2, "Beloved, I pray that you may prosper in all things and be in health, just as your soul prospers." We can infer that one's prosperity is directly linked to the stability and flourishing of one's soul.

As children of God, we know that we are primarily spirits, we live in our bodies and we have souls, 1 Thessalonians 5:23.

So according to this scripture, I am a spirit, I have a soul, and I live in a body. With my spirit, I connect with the supernatural. The soul has been described as the central control valve, the seat of reasoning, thinking, feelings/emotions and decision-making. With my body, I relate to the physical world and carry out the dictates of my mind.

God created us and He knows all about us and how we function: spiritually, psychologically (the soul), and physically (the body). There is no aspect of me, as an individual that is hidden from God, Psalm 139:15. God's original intention for mankind was perfection, Genesis 1: 31, God saw everything that He had made and indeed it was very good. But the fall of mankind happened in Genesis Chapter 3 and it affected man in all dimensions:

- Spiritual death.

- Impact on the soul, leading to negative orientations, weakness of the mind and emotions and generally with a tendency to work against the plan of God, Romans 8: 6-7.

- Impact on the body, leading to all sorts of physical health issues.

We know the story of redemption very well, our Lord and Savior came to earth and redeemed us back to God, with the plan of redeeming us back to the Father's original plan.

There has been a lot of emphasis in the body of Christ on the spiritual aspect and so it should be because according to the opening statement, it is the strong spirit of a man that sustains in times of adversity. And with the rising challenge on the physical body, in the secular world and also, in the body of Christ, we have also put a lot of emphasis on the need to take care of our bodies. A significant amount of wealth has been and continues to be spent on the need to eat well and exercise to reduce the risk of having chronic physical health conditions e.g. obesity, type 2 diabetes, dementia, cancer, etc.

We have not put the same amount of effort or resources into educating people about the need to address the issues of the soul (mind and emotional wellbeing). The state of a man's soul becomes more apparent at a time of crisis or adversity. As mentioned above, one's prosperity and overall health are dependent on the prosperity of one's soul. It is, therefore, crucial that we begin to give attention to the state of our souls. As you spend time to develop yourself spiritually, to look after your physical health by ensuring that you eat the right kind of food and exercise as well as going for certain health checks, it is equally prudent to invest the same amount of resources, energy, and time to look after the state of your soul.

How do I begin to do this?

It is imperative that you, as an individual, are aware of the state of your soul. The fact that you are a Christian does not mean that all is well with the state of your soul, the same way that you cannot neglect the state of your body. Many of us spend time ensuring that we take adequate care of our bodies. Remember what I said earlier on, the fall of mankind affected all human dimensions, the spirit, the soul, and the body. For the spirit to be restored back to the original position God intended, you had to make a quality decision to become a child of God by repenting and asking God to come into your life, however, this was just the beginning of the journey. After this initial step, you were given a task, according to 1 Peter 2:2, "as newborn babes, desire the pure milk of the Word that you may grow thereby." This means that the extent of your spiritual growth is entirely dependent on you, as an individual. Remember, this is the spiritual aspect of you hence requires your on-going craving and desire for the Word to ensure your continued spiritual growth.

With regard to the soul, Romans 12:2, says, "do not conform to the pattern of this world, but be transformed by the renewing of your mind." This scripture implies that your transformation, as an individual, will take place through the renewing of the mind. This is a process that will involve me, as an individual, taking necessary steps. It involves me ensuring that I do not respond the way the world does and I must continually engage in the process to bring my reasoning/thinking style, emotions, and decision-making, in line with God's way. The fact that it is a process also means that I will continue to take the necessary steps to ensure that I do not respond to things this year the way I did last year. I must continually see a change in the way that I respond to or deal with things.

The same way the Bible encourages us to grow spiritually, we are also a work-in-progress, in regard to the area of our soul; the seat of reasoning/thinking, emotions/feelings, and decision-making.

Cognition (Thinking) ------Emotions (Feelings) ------ Action (Behaviour)

According to Cognitive Behaviour Therapy Principles, the way we think affects the way we feel, which in turns affects the way we behave. This is corroborated by the Bible, in Proverbs 23:7, "as he thinks in his heart, so is he." This means that if one has a negative thinking style, it can be a major trigger to the way one responds to stress, and ultimately, affects the way one behaves, in crisis or when faced with stress.

In order to understand this better, it will be helpful to look at the things that affect how we become who we are in terms of our personality, that is, the unique, 'you', which determines the following:

- The way you relate to people

- The way you manage your emotions

- The way you think generally about things, what we refer to as your thinking style

- The way you perceive the world, yourself, and yourself in relation to other people.

The development of one's personality is a combination of genes (nature) and early childhood experiences (nurture). An interaction between what we have brought into this world in terms of our genetic makeup (nature) and the environment in which we have been nurtured is important in terms of the development of one's personality. Negative early life experiences or negative interactions with the main caregiver(s) can, adversely, impact the body's stress response. The experience one has as a child can predict one's response to stress, i.e., one's body stress response is primed by early childhood experiences.

If one is born with a genetic predisposition of being easily overwhelmed or startled by things around (difficult temperament), but is fortunate enough to have an uneventful and good childhood, as well as good nurturing environment, and is being looked after by carers who are easily available and attuned to one's needs, one is likely to develop a good sense of self, as well as a good sense of one's self in relation to others. This is likely to translate into a better perception of self and of the world, as well as impact on the way one relates to others, and responds to any adverse life events. The final result in terms of one's childhood is a secure sense of self, positive internal working model, and a generally positive outlook on the world. It forms a good foundation in terms of being able to be self-aware, be emotionally resourceful, and able to manage or control one's emotions.

On the other hand, if one is already born with challenges in the area of one's temperament and then suffered a major childhood adversity like abuse of any form or loss, in terms of death of a parent, parental separation/divorce, leading to loss of attachment or dysfunctional attachment with a caregiver, this is likely to have a major blow on the sense of self, which ultimately, affects one's perception of oneself, how one relates to others as well as one's perception of the world in general. This experience would have been stressful and damaging if the body's stress system is not provided with help/support to recover, thereby priming the body's stress response system in a negative way. This will affect how the individual responds to future stressful events.

In summary, the body's stress response system is affected by how much early stress it has to deal with, in the form of early childhood adversity and how well the system is helped to recover. When one is well resourced, in terms of one's genetic makeup and well nurtured, i.e. the necessary support and care is given during childhood, then one develops into an adult who is able to self-soothe and manage emotions better during the time of crisis.

The personality, the unique, 'you', a combination of your genes (temperament) and early experiences (both in terms of childhood traumatic events and the environment) can impact on the way you, as an individual, respond to stress and react in a time of crisis or adversity.

Certain personalities can increase the likelihood of developing certain mental health issues or disorders in the same manner that certain risk factors can increase the likelihood of having certain physical health problems. For example, obesity is linked to diabetes mellitus.

Can I ask you some questions; are you aware of the unique, 'you'?

- Do you have a tendency to worry all the time, 'anxious prone personality'?
- Are you a perfectionist?
- Do you tend to procrastinate?
- Are you a happy-go-lucky individual?
- Do you avoid dealing with things or do you live in denial?

Is there a family history of mental health-related issues, because we know that mental health problems tend to run in the family? Have you researched other things that, in addition to this genetic vulnerability, can affect the way you respond to things?

Have you experienced any trauma during childhood, for example, abuse, whether physical, emotional, or sexual, the death of any loved one, parental conflicts, separation, or divorce?

If the answer to any of the above questions is yes, have you addressed this in any way by seeking professional help, because if not, there is a possibility that this could impact on how you respond to any form of crisis or stress.

Anything that threatens or impacts on one's emotional security during childhood is likely to have a negative effect on the body's stress response system and how one responds to stress or any negative event as an adult.

This can lead to 2 extremes in terms of response to stress:

- On the one hand, leading to individuals with high level of production of stress hormones with the slightest provocation, thereby becoming easily depressed, easily anxious, and prone to negative action or behaviour like overeating.

- On the other extreme, leading to individuals with minimal or no outward response to stress, this individual has learnt to avoid getting in touch with their emotions.

The same way you go for a routine, physical health check, you need to regularly check the state of your mind and emotions and promptly deal with things.

How self-aware are you, in terms of your emotional response? Are you a high reactor to stress, i.e., do you have a tendency to produce a high level of stress hormones with the slightest provocation? Or are you a low or no reactor to stress, i.e. is your body's stress response subdued?

Remember, the strong spirit of a man sustains him in the time of adversity. If you start with a strong spirit, you are likely to be in a better position to fight effectively and win. In the same vein, if you have already invested time and resources in ensuring that you have a better understanding of your mind, emotional state, and how you respond to stress, you will be in a better position to know what to do during the time of crisis and you are likely to respond to things better. The same applies to your physical health; you are more likely to recover quickly if you are in a better physically, healthy state when an infection strikes.

The learning from the above is this: it is important where you are starting, therefore be aware of the state of your mind and your emotional state.

Now let us now focus on Emotional Intelligence

The American Heritage Science Dictionary defines **emotion** as a psychological (mental) state that arises spontaneously rather than through conscious effort and is sometimes accompanied by physiological (physical) changes.

Collins Dictionary defines it as a feeling of happiness, love, anger, and hatred, fear, which can be caused by the people you are with or the situation you are in. It is the part of a person's character (the part of the unique, 'you') that consists of their feelings, as opposed to their thoughts.

Looking at these two definitions, we can see that emotions can arise suddenly, i.e. without any external cause or in the context of one's relationship with others or as a result of environmental reason.

Emotion can either be positive or negative. Every emotion has its purpose; it can alert one to the state of one's inner world.

Intelligence, on the other hand, is defined as the ability to **acquire, understand,** and **use knowledge** appropriately.

For example, if someone has a tendency to worry excessively or finds him/herself experiencing symptoms of anxiety or displaying other strong and negative emotions repeatedly and it's impacting on his/her health or relationship with others, it is not wise to neglect it and say, that's just who I am. Someone who is seeking to be emotionally intelligent will seek to know why, and what needs to be done.

The Psychologists define emotional intelligence as an **awareness of one's** emotions and those of others in the context of managing and relating with others.

Out of balance emotions, in either way, can lead to mayhem in one's individual life and has the potential to have a significant impact in terms of having a successful relationship or career. It can become pathological and undermine stability, both in terms of one's individual life and relationship with others.

What are some of the causes of extreme display of emotions?

- Underlying vulnerability, in terms of one's genetic makeup, as mentioned above, a 'highly reactive or overly sensitive individual versus a less reactive individual'.

- Unresolved traumatic childhood experiences.

- Recent life events, like divorce, financial problems, unemployment, relationship problems, health issues, etc.

You can have two individuals going through the same stressful events and the two of them are likely to respond differently, why? The answer lies in the starting point, in terms of the states of their minds and emotional well-being as well as their unique personality style, 'a high or low reactor to stress'.

What happens to us when we feel stressed, that is when we have too many demands placed on us, or when we have no control over what happens to us? This might be in the context of the following:

- Our job, work-related stress,

- Our role as parents, especially when the role places more demands on us, (physically, emotionally, or financially) as children go through different stages of life,

- Relationship difficulties, leading to separation or divorce,

- Financial difficulties, struggling to make ends meet, or dealing with debts,

- Unemployment or repeated loss of jobs,

- Immigration problems,

- Health issues, i.e., challenges with one's health.

When one is stressed, the body's stress response system is activated leading to release of the stress hormones, which is one's body's way of preparing one to respond to what the body perceives as a threat. How the body responds depends on how the stress response system had been previously primed during childhood.

As mentioned above, we all have our unique way of responding to stress, depending on how much early stress one has had to deal with and how well the stress response system has been helped to recover. This is the reason we see different people respond to stressful life events differently. This also affects the process of adjustment and recovery from such life events.

Persistent and high level of the stress hormones has a negative effect on one's physical and emotional well-being. Stress has been linked to chronic pain, digestive problems, weight problems, high blood pressure, as well as increased vulnerability to having an infection, to name but a few.

In terms of emotional well-being, stress has been linked with sleep problems as well as mood disorders like anxiety and depression.

How do I deal with stress triggered by traumatic events?

- Avoid dealing with emotional issues by engaging in unhealthy physical things, like overeating. This is likely to lead to weight gain and worsens poor self-esteem and confidence, ultimately, leading to increased level of anxiety and depression.

- Do not spend money that you do not have, buying more things that you do not need or spending more money on yourself that you do not have will only provide temporary relief but will not provide a lasting solution. It will lead to more debts and make the situation worse.

So what do I do?

There are three areas to address: identify the source of the stress, look at your reaction, and identify what it is about you, as an individual, that is making you respond the way you are.

Myself: What is it about myself that has led me to respond to this situation like this? What has this taught me about myself, am I a high or low reactor to stress? What have I learnt about my unique way of responding to stress? Have I discovered anything about myself in terms of my genetic makeup or things that I have not addressed about my past that have now predisposed me to respond to this event the way that I have?

Secondly, I need to seek professional help to disentangle the emotional response that belongs to the current life events and those that belong to issues from the past. For example, is the emotional response to the current loss or crisis a combination of the issues from the past and that of the current ones? Or is there something about my personality or issues from the past that is stopping me from making a decision about an abusive relationship, leading to me feeling stuck? Some people remain in an abusive relationship because of poor sense of self; they feel that is all they deserve, hence refuse to take the necessary action that will change the situation.

Thirdly, once I have addressed the above and I am on the right path, I need to make quality decisions to begin to look after myself by eating healthily, getting adequate sleep, making time to relax and rest, and engaging with the right support network. You deserve that, 'me' time and are worthy of the resources that you spend on yourself. Do not believe those lies that keep going through your mind about yourself. These are called negative automatic thoughts, they pop into your mind without any invitation, and they can trigger a display of extreme emotions. The Bible says in Psalm 139: 14, you are "fearfully and wonderfully made." You are God's handiwork hence you are marvellous. According to the Dictionary, the word "marvellous" means amazingly impressive, spectacular, and stunning. Start focusing your mind on the person God says you are.

The Situation: Remember, stress occurs when we are unable to cope with demands or when we have no control over the situation hence you need to ask yourself honest questions like, what can I do to change the situation? Can I re-train, in the case of n unemployment situation? Can we go for counselling as a couple in the case of a relationship problem? Can I seek professional help if I am struggling as a parent?

Or can you accept what you cannot change, for example, if you work full time, then maybe you need to accept that you cannot accept every invitation to school sporting activities or school events and need to share this with your spouse?

Or maybe, you need to learn to say no and stop overcommitting yourself. Perhaps, you find it difficult to say no because of unresolved issues from the past. Do you have a tendency to overcommit because of fear of rejection and abandonment or do you do this as an exchange for their love?

My Reaction: What can I do about the way I react to the situation? In order for me to know what to do, I need to be aware of my own emotional response to people and situations. This takes us back to the issue of being emotionally intelligent – being aware of one's thoughts, which can affect one's emotional response and behaviour – the way I think, affects the way I feel and ultimately, my behaviour.

This brings us to the issue of being self-aware. I cannot make progress unless I am aware of my starting point and then learn ways to change what needs changing, acquire the necessary skills to keep advancing, and re-evaluating myself as I continue on my journey.

Self-Awareness

- Recognise the feelings/emotions, do not avoid or disregard them.

- Ask questions. For example, What has triggered this? Has it been triggered by negative/anxious thoughts about the future or self-belittling thoughts?

- Can you see the link between the negative thought patterns and the feelings, for example, of anxiety, despair or depression, and the behaviour, for example, eating unhealthy food, avoiding others, or engaging in desperate measures?

- Are you able to identify the consequences, both short-term and long-term ones? If you carry on with the same pattern of behaviour, what is likely to happen? Would things change for the better or would they get worse? If I carry on overeating, leading to weight gain, what would happen to my sense of self and confidence and would this have a further impact on the existing relationship problem? If I keep spending money, what impact would that have on the already stretched family finances?

- Once you have been able to identify the consequences, either on your own or with the help of someone else, a trusted friend, or professional, can you start thinking about alternatives and the possible benefits? You might need to agree to a plan that is realistic and achievable and hold yourself accountable.

- Not everything about you, as a person, is negative. Can you identify any strength in yourself or anything that you are good at doing? You might be going through a challenge in a particular area, for example in your relationship, but can you see other areas of your life where you are doing well, for example, a loving mother, a good listener or someone who has made progress in terms of their career? This changes the focus in terms of how you see yourself, which affects the way you see the situation you are facing and other people around you. One's emotional response to any situation is usually affected by one's perception of oneself.

By focusing one's energy not only on the negative but also on one's strength, one can alter one's attitude and behaviour. For example, the fact that I am going through this situation does not mean I am a failure; the totality of who I am is not defined by this life event. This, immediately, alters the negative thinking style of, ' I am a failure, or I am less than others because of what I am going through.' This eventually affects the way you feel about yourself, the situation, and your behaviour. You begin to see yourself as someone who is valuable, you no longer see the need to stuff yourself with food that your body does not need, or engage in any unhealthy ways to manage negative emotions.

Final words

It is God's will for you to prosper in your soul, according to 3 John 3:2.

The Dictionary defines prosperity as; to flourish, to grow strong, and healthy. It is His will that you flourish in your soul (mind, emotion) and that you become emotionally strong and healthy. This is God's plan for you as an individual. Things might have gone wrong because of what happened in the past, during your childhood, and primed you to respond in a particular way to stress. It does not have to continue to be so; you can make a decision to co-operate with God and His Word and begin to change the way your mind has been programmed to respond to stress and life events. In the same way, a newborn spiritual babe has to desire/crave the Word, to grow spiritually (1 Peter 2:2), you have a responsibility to do something to ensure the growth or flourishing of your mind/emotional state.

God might lead you to seek professional help in the first instance to have an understanding of why you are the way you are or respond to things the way you do and to learn ways to manage the negative emotions triggered by the stressful life events.

The Word of God is full of scriptures that you can begin to focus your mind on. For example in Philippians 4:8, the Word of God tells us what to focus our minds on.

God is faithful and He will see you through. You will come out on the other side as a better individual if you will allow your heavenly Father to take you through the process of self-discovery and transformation. Your best days are ahead of you.

AUTHOR'S CONCLUSION

As mentioned at the beginning of this book, my heart's desire in writing this book is to encourage you and let you know that regardless of your challenges, you can still live your life to the fullest. If I can do it, you can do it too. I trust this book has given you the tools you need to bounce back in the face of adversity and be the best version of you. Like you, I'm still a work-in-progress, but my determination not to give up on myself during those trying times is what has brought me this far.

Leave the past behind and look forward to the glorious future that is ahead of you. Take the necessary steps needed during the difficult seasons so you can come out victorious.

My aim is to continue to put into practice everything I've written in this book so my life can continue to be a blessing to many. One of my future goals is to open a Refresh Centre for women. This will be a place of respite for women that are facing different challenges and need a place just to offload their burdens. Women Empowering Projects vision has enlightened me that there are a lot of women out there struggling with how to overcome adversity without losing themselves in the process. I want to make myself available and be able to offer this service.

I encourage you to launch out to fulfil whatever passion you have that is still locked within. Be bold and take the baby steps, and you will be amazed at how far you can go. I'm cheering you on!

Shalom
Grateful Rachel

ABOUT THE AUTHOR

Grateful Rachel is a mother of two amazing boys. She is also a qualified teacher and has been successfully running a tuition centre since 2005. Her passion for women developed over the years; she is known to be a source of strength and support for women who face varying challenges in their lives. She is the founder of Women Empowering Projects, a non-profit organisation that aims to provide a place of respite where women come to be elevated above their challenges, inspired to be the change, and rejuvenated for life's journey. She has successfully organised various events to bring like-minded women together to encourage and support them at different levels. In her spare time, she loves shopping, travelling, going out, and meeting new people.

You can connect with Grateful Rachel by visiting her website, www.womenempoweringprojects.org

Book Synopsis

This book tells a story of victory against painful odds. Grateful Rachel has gone through extremely difficult circumstances. At only 8 years old, she discovered that the woman she called, "mum," was actually, her grandmother. At 17, she finally reunited with the rest of her family, but her joy was short-lived as her father died seven months after this happy reunion. Her heart was broken, the loss and trauma from such a painful childhood made life unbearable. Determined not to give up, she carried on and got married and had two wonderful sons, yet after 19 years of working through a difficult marriage, it ended in a divorce. Yet today, she is an accomplished woman and is living her best life yet.

Grateful Rachel's story is a true life story of bouncing back and standing firm in the face of adversity. In this book, she shares her powerful testimony and how she was able to overcome her trials and turn them into triumphs. This book has practical tips and advice on how you, too, can rise above the challenges in life and bounce back so you can become the person you were created to be.